**THAT'S LIFE
PictureStories**

BOOK 1
Emergency

Tana Reiff

LAKE EDUCATION
Belmont, California

Cover Design: Ina McInnis
Text Designer: Diann Abbott

Copyright © 1995 by Lake Education, a division of Lake Publishing Company, 500 Harbor Blvd., Belmont, CA 94002. All rights reserved. No part of this book may be reproduced by any means, transmitted, or translated into a machine language without written permission from the publisher.

Library of Congress Catalog Number: 94-079117

ISBN 1-56103-776-1

Printed in the United States of America

1 9 8 7 6 5 4 3 2 1

The Marcianos

- **Frank Marciano** *He owns a grocery store and has something to say on every subject.*
- **Marge Marciano** *She listens to everyone's problems and knows how to help.*
- **Ernesto Marciano** *Frank's father retires from life until he meets Rosa Esteban.*
- **Gina Marciano** *The Marcianos' daughter is very much her own woman.*
- **Doug Kelly** *He and Gina Marciano have a life plan that works for them.*

The Adamses

- **Walter Adams** *Keeping up with a growing family has its problems.*
- **Ruth Adams** *She manages to keep her cool through all of life's surprises.*
- **Pat Adams** *A 13-year-old learns something new about life every day.*
- **Tyrone Adams** *At 16, does "Mr. Basketball" really know it all?*

The Estebans

- **Carlos Esteban** *Since his wife's death, he's both father and mother to his children.*
- **Rosa Esteban** *Carlos's mother doesn't let age stand in the way of happiness.*
- **Rick Esteban** *He finds that it's easy to get in trouble when you're 16.*
- **Roberto Esteban** *This 14-year-old boy is making big plans for his future.*
- **Bonita Esteban** *Growing up means having to learn about all sides of life.*

The Nguyens

- **Nguyen Lan** *She can handle being a single parent in a new country.*
- **Nguyen Tam** *At 4, he asks his mother why he has no father at home.*

Don Kaufman tells about himself

Don Kaufman here. I bring mail to this street. Been doing it for 7 years. Started when I was 26. I love it. I also like to write. This job gives me ideas. Like with Frank and Marge Marciano. They had a hard time up there the other day.

Meet Don Kaufman. He brings mail to this street. He began delivering mail seven years ago. He was 26 then. Don loves his job. He also likes to write. His job gives him ideas to write about. Don hears Frank and Marge Marciano arguing a lot. They had a hard time the other day.

Do you sometimes argue with other people?
What do you argue about?

Frank Marciano thinks it's the end for him

Frank has to go to the hospital. He is going in an ambulance. He won't stop talking the whole way to the hospital. Marge tries to make him stop. Frank still does not stop talking. He says he is going to die. Marge tells him he will be all right.

"This isn't a heart attack," says the paramedic. "You are just fine."

What kind of person do you think Frank is?

A parade blocks the street

"If I'm fine," says Frank, "why am I going to a hospital?"

"Just to be sure," says the paramedic. At that moment the ambulance runs into a parade. It is a school parade. The ambulance cannot move.

How do you feel when you have to wait for something?

Frank is not ready for a parade

The people in the parade do not move out of the way. They cannot hear the siren. The band is too loud. The ambulance driver and the paramedic are talking about the parade.

"I'm going to die," cries Frank. "And they want to watch a parade!"

"Go up to 10th Street," says Marge to the driver. "You can get across there."

Suppose you are Frank. What is going on in your head right now?

What about driving up another street?

Frank can hear the band. It is very noisy. The ambulance just sits there. It still cannot get past the parade.

The paramedic and the driver talk about going up 10th Street. That will add six or seven minutes to the trip.

What would you do if you were the driver?

The paramedic hears his school fight song

Frank wants to turn around. He wants to go up 10th Street. He wants to get to the hospital as soon as possible.

Marge tells Frank to calm down. She is afraid he will have a heart attack.

Just then the parade passes them. The ambulance can move again. The paramedic hears the band playing. They are playing his school fight song!

Think of an old song. Why do you think you remember it?

Waiting makes Frank boil over

Frank just wants to get to the hospital. He is not being calm. *"Marge!"* he screams.

In your own words, what does it mean to "boil over"?

The whole neighborhood is talking

18

Kaufman says everyone is talking about Frank. The hospital still doesn't know what's wrong with him.

Ruth Adams lives around the corner from the Marcianos'. Her husband's name is Walter. They have two kids. Kaufman just saw Ruth heading for the Marcianos'. She is going to ask Marge what is happening with Frank.

How does Kaufman know that everyone is talking about Frank?

Ruth Adams hears that it was a false alarm

Ruth Adams goes to see Marge. She wants to know how Frank is doing.

"Well, he's still in the hospital," says Marge. "Maybe just for the night. They want to run some tests. They think it's his gall bladder."

"I heard he had a heart attack," says Ruth.

Marge says that Frank thought it was a heart attack, too. Many people make the same mistake. They think a gall bladder attack is a heart attack.

Suppose you think you are having a heart attack. What would you do?

Marge Marciano will run the grocery store

Ruth asks if Marge will close the grocery store since Frank is sick.

"Are you kidding?" laughs Marge. "We have a Ma and Pa store. We can't close! I can take care of things. But I could sure use Tyrone's help."

Ruth says that her son Tyrone can help Marge. Then Ruth begins to laugh. "I'm sorry," she says. "I just have this picture of Frank thinking he's having a heart attack!"

Why do you think Ruth is laughing?

It's no laughing matter, but. . . .

Marge begins to laugh with Ruth. "You should have seen him, Ruth," she says. She tells about how Frank had been in the ambulance. He had been very upset. He had yelled at the men. He had even called them "quacks."

Would you like to have a neighbor like Ruth?

Nguyen Lan shops for food

Mrs. Nguyen Lan is another neighbor. She comes into the store to buy soup and soda. Frank is back at work. He tells Nguyen Lan about returnable bottles. Lan can bring back her empty soda bottles. Then Frank will return the deposit she paid for them.

What is another good reason to return bottles?

Lan doesn't need Tyrone Adams's help

Nguyen Lan wants to save money. Food costs so much. Frank says Lan should grow her own food.

Lan starts to pick up her grocery bag. Frank asks Tyrone to give her a hand. "That's OK," says Lan. "I can carry my own bags."

What ways do you know to save money on food?

Tyrone's job is to stack cans

Nguyen Lan leaves the store. Frank says "So long!" to her. Then he goes over to see what Tyrone is doing.

Tyrone is making a stack of dog food cans. He wants to use every can. But he will have to start over again. He has seven cans left over.

When was the last time you had to start something over?

Sometimes Frank tries to help

Frank has an idea. He wants to use the seven cans that are left over. He wants to help Tyrone. So Frank tries to fix the stack. Instead, he knocks it over. Tyrone tries to stop Frank. But it is too late. There are cans all over the floor.

What would you say to Frank if you were Tyrone?

The cans on the floor surprise Marge

Frank begins picking up the cans. But Tyrone wants to do it himself. He tells Frank to go cut up chickens instead.

Just then Marge comes into the store. She sees the cans all over the floor. Then she asks how Frank feels.

"Fine," says Frank. "No pain at all. Those pills really help!"

Do you believe everything is really OK with Frank?

Frank knows he shouldn't eat salami

Frank's mouth begins to move. Marge sees it. She asks Frank what he is eating.

"I'm not eating," says Frank. But Frank *is* eating. He is eating a piece of salami. He took it out of the meat case. Marge knows that the doctor told Frank not to eat salami. Frank tells Marge not to worry about him. "I know what I'm doing!" he says.

Do you know anyone like Frank? How is that person like Frank?

Kaufman has some ideas about people

"Famous last words!" says Don Kaufman. Kaufman has heard what Frank said. "It's a funny thing about people," Kaufman goes on. "They say they won't do something again. But they do it anyway. But you pay a price, as Frank found out. Well, that's life."

What is something that you have "paid a price" for?

Walter Adams needs his hedge trimmers back

Walter Adams comes over to the Marcianos'. He wants to get his hedge trimmers. Last week he loaned them to Frank. Now he needs to trim some bushes. Marge is working on store business.

"I'll get them," says Marge. "I should have given them back already."

Do you have something that you should give back to someone?

It sounds like trouble again

Marge says she has trimmed the hedge herself. Frank isn't very good at yard work. Walter says she has done a good job.

Then all of a sudden, Marge and Walter hear a loud scream. *"Marge! Come quick!"*

Which do you like better—outside work or inside work?

A second attack for Frank

The scream is from Frank. He is having another attack. He should have done what the doctor told him to do.

Marge wants to call a doctor. But Walter has a different idea. Walter thinks he and Marge should take Frank right to the hospital.

What would you do first at a time like this—call a doctor or take someone right to the hospital?

Marge makes an emergency call

I'd better call first and see what to do till we get help. Oh, where is that number?

Let me look. Dr. Nelson?

Right. 555-0780. Hello? This is Marge Marciano. I think my husband's having a gall bladder attack. Oh, the doctor's not in? Right.... Walter, we must call an ambulance.

Marge wants to call a doctor first. She wants to call Dr. Nelson. The doctor can tell them what to do. Marge finds the telephone number. Then she makes the call. Dr. Nelson is not there. Marge and Walter will have to call an ambulance.

How do you call an ambulance in your town?

Get an ambulance here quick!

MARGE!

I'll call. You go with Frank.

The number is above the phone.

Here it is.

Hello, this is an emergency. We need an ambulance at 216 Pine Drive. 2 blocks south of Wilson Boulevard. My name is Walter Adams. The sick person here is Frank Marciano.

Marge goes to check on Frank. Walter calls the ambulance. The number is above the telephone.

"Hello," says Walter. "This is an emergency. We need an ambulance at 216 Pine Drive. My name is Walter Adams. The sick person is Frank Marciano."

Where do you keep emergency telephone numbers?

Frank finally gets to the emergency room

"You sure this is the emergency room? It's more like a morgue. Are they just letting me die?"

"I'm sure someone will be here soon."

"Mr. Marciano? What's the problem here?"

"The problem is that I'm dying."

The ambulance takes Frank to the hospital. He waits in the emergency room. It seems like a long wait.

At last a nurse comes into the room. "Mr. Marciano?" asks the nurse. "What's the problem here?"

"The problem is that I'm dying!" cries Frank.

What do you think will happen to Frank?

Trouble with the nurse

"So you are dying?" says the nurse. "Then I am your lifesaver."

"Well, you *are* kind of round," says Frank.

Marge does not think Frank's joke is funny. She goes on to tell the nurse about Frank's gall bladder. Frank is trying to take out the thermometer. "Don't take that out!" says the nurse. "And let me check your heartbeat."

Do you know anyone who has saved a life?

All Frank's signs seem normal to the nurse

Frank is really in pain. Marge asks for pain pills for him.

"Not right now," says the nurse. "Put that thermometer back, Mr. Marciano! Well, his heart is OK." Then she takes Frank's blood pressure. It is OK, too.

Where can you get a blood pressure check?

Frank doesn't think pain is normal

The nurse tells Frank his temperature is OK. It is 98.6. "And the pain is OK, too," says the nurse.

"Did you hear that, Marge?" asks Frank. "The pain is OK?" Frank does not *feel* OK.

"You asked for it," says Marge. "You had to make that crack about her size!"

What do you do when someone makes a joke about you?

A talk with Dr. Williams

A doctor comes in. It is Dr. Williams, not Dr. Nelson. But he knows all about Frank's gall bladder problems. Frank will have to have some tests. He will have to stay in the hospital tonight. He might even have to stay longer.

"Do I need surgery?" asks Frank. He doesn't like the idea.

Have you ever stayed in a hospital? What was it like?

Some tests will have to be run

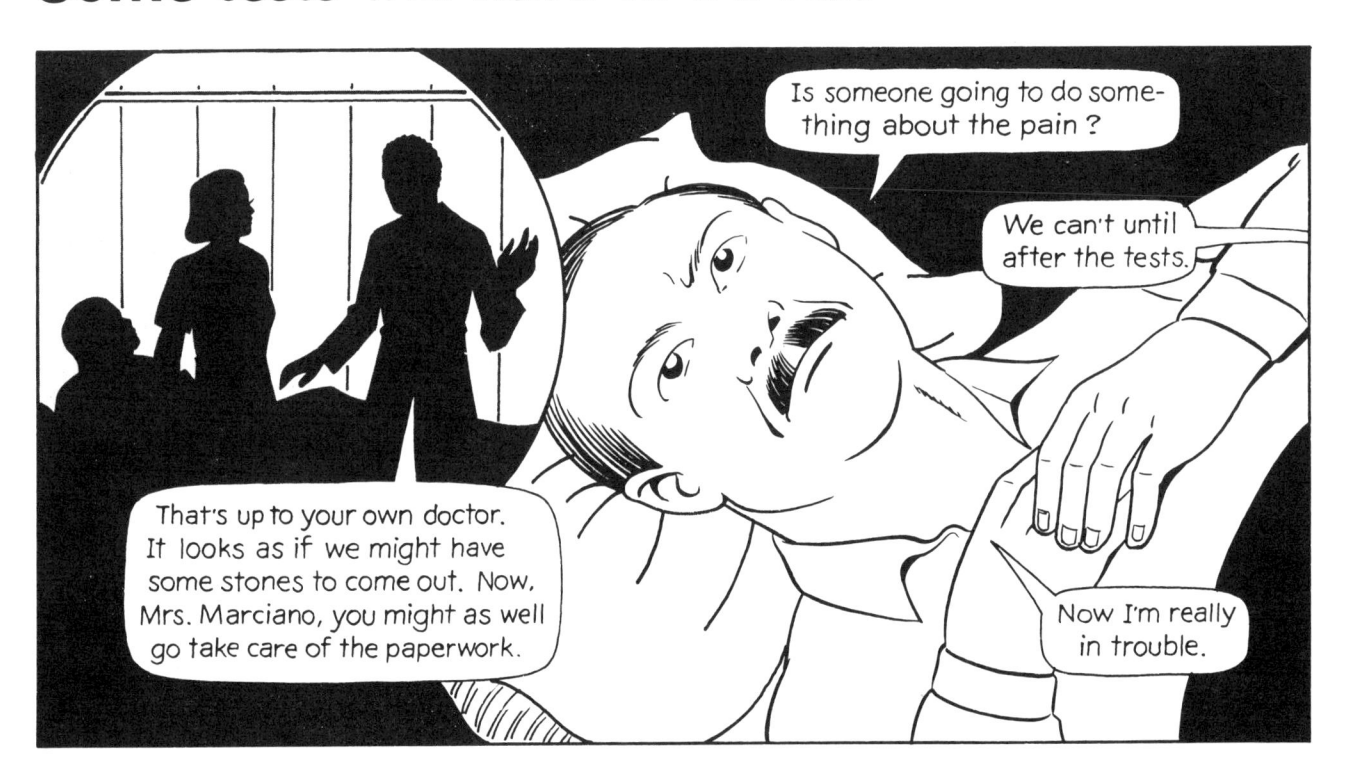

Dr. Williams cannot tell Frank about surgery. Dr. Nelson will have to decide about that. But there is a good chance that Frank has gallstones.

Marge leaves to take care of the paperwork.

"Is someone going to do something about the pain?" asks Frank.

"We can't until after the tests," says Dr. Williams.

"Now I'm really in trouble," says Frank.

What's the most painful thing that ever happened to you?

Kaufman wonders about the word *hospital*

So Frank is back in the hospital. Hospital. I must find out where that word came from. Frank has a few problems. But so does Marge. Filling out forms can be a real problem.

Frank is back in the hospital. The word *hospital* is interesting. Kaufman wants to find out where the word comes from. Anyway, Frank has some problems. But so does Marge. She is the one who is filling out the forms. The hospital needs these forms, but filling them out can be a real problem.

How do you feel about filling out forms?

Marge takes care of the paperwork

A woman asks Marge questions. She will put this information on hospital forms. Marge gives Frank's telephone number, birth date, and other facts. She gives the woman all the information needed.

Just then Ruth Adams comes up. "Marge!" says Ruth. "How's Frank?"

Why has Ruth come to the hospital?

A helping hand from Walter

Marge tells Ruth all about Frank. She says that he has had another attack. The doctors are giving him tests. Then Marge and Ruth go for coffee.

"I'm glad Walter was there when Frank got sick," says Marge.

Ruth laughs. "Walt was never too good with sick people!"

What can you do to help sick people?

Frank doesn't take it lying down

Marge and Ruth go to find Frank. "Hi, Frank!" says Marge. "How are you?"

"First they stuck me," says Frank. "Now they put me here in the hall. This is all too much."

At last someone comes to get Frank. "When I die, Walter can have my Big Band records," says Frank. Marge just wishes Frank had stuck to the diet. If he had, maybe he wouldn't be so sick now.

Do you think Frank is more angry or afraid?

Thinking about medical costs

Marge and Ruth are talking again. Marge is afraid Frank will need surgery. She doesn't like the idea.

"My brother's wife had gallstones," says Ruth. "Just the doctor's bill alone cost a fortune."

"Oh, no!" Marge cries. "Our insurance won't cover all of it. We have to buy low-cost insurance. And the hospital bill will be even more!" Marge can see a whole new set of problems ahead.

What health insurance do you have? What does it cover?

Health insurance can be a big help

Walter is a member of a union. The union has group insurance. The hospital insurance takes care of the whole Adams family. But Frank works for himself. He and Marge buy their own insurance. They are not part of a group plan.

Then Dr. Nelson comes in. She sits down with Ruth and Marge. "No coffee for me," says Dr. Nelson. "My doctor limits me to three cups a day."

Do you drink too much coffee? If so, how could you cut down?

Frank will probably need surgery

Dr. Nelson says Frank is still having tests. He will probably need surgery. He must stay in the hospital tonight.

"Is it that bad?" asks Marge. "Does Frank know yet?"

"Let's wait till after the tests," says Dr. Nelson. "We'll tell him then. Nothing is sure yet."

When would you tell Frank that he might need surgery?

Kaufman tells about the Marcianos' children

"I don't want to talk too loud here in the library. Now... Frank and Marge have 2 children. Paul's about 30... lives overseas... and Gina... nice girl."

"She's a buyer in a department store. When Gina left for school, Frank was a mess. Marge... she's a rock. Now Frank, they'll love him at the hospital. By the way, "hospital" means "bedroom." But I don't think Frank saw it that way."

Kaufman is looking up the word *hospital*. He tells us more about the Marciano family. Frank and Marge have two children. Paul is about 30. He does not live in this country. Gina is 25. She is a buyer for a big store.

Kaufman says the word *hospital* means the same as *bedroom*. Kaufman doesn't think Frank sees it that way.

How would you like being in a hospital?

A private talk with Marge

The tests are over. Frank must have surgery. He must have his gall bladder taken out. Marge goes to talk to Frank. A nurse is in his room. The nurse is trying to make him feel better. Marge tries to make him feel better, too.

The surgery will be at 8:30 A.M. That is just 12 hours away.

Frank asks Marge to come closer. He wants to have a private talk with her.

What could you do to help someone in pain?

Marge talks about visiting the bank

"Don't worry about the money," Marge tells Frank. "I'm going to the bank tomorrow. We must pay the first $500. Then our insurance will pay 80% of the rest."

"We'll still have to pay our 20%," says Frank.

"I'll talk to Mr. Lightfoot about a loan," says Marge. "We can put up our car for a loan."

Suppose you need a loan. What could you "put up" for it?

Would a medical school buy Frank's body?

Frank thinks the car is too old. Besides, they will soon need money to fix up a room in their house. Frank's father will be moving in with them soon.

"Things will be fine," says Marge. "Now get some rest. I love you." She kisses Frank.

"Marge!" says Frank. "Find out if you can sell my body to a medical school after I die. See you in the morning . . . I hope!"

Do you think Frank will be OK?

Mr. Lightfoot figures out a bank loan

Marge goes to the bank. She talks to Mr. Lightfoot. She wants to know about the interest rate.

"I'm sure our bank can help you," says Mr. Lightfoot. "You will need a loan of about $1,500. The interest will be 10%."

Why do you think Marge asks how much the interest will be?

Marge can borrow against their house

"What can we put up for the loan?" asks Marge. "Our car is too old."

Mr. Lightfoot says they can put up their home. Marge and Frank did not think of doing that. Getting a loan will not be so hard after all. Marge leaves the bank then. She goes to the hospital. She wants to tell Frank about the loan.

Have you ever asked for a loan? What happened?

A way to pay hospital bills without interest

Frank's surgery is over. He is getting better fast.

Marge goes back to the hospital. Then she finds out about another way to help pay their bills. The hospital has a plan. Frank and Marge can make part-payments for four months. They will not be charged interest on these payments. Marge tells Frank about this plan. They will still need $1,000. They can get that much from the bank.

What do you think of this new plan?

Time for Marge to plan a budget

"We have to make some changes," Marge says. She is talking about money. "No more 60¢ cigars. And we must find ways to save more money."

"Or we could buy more insurance," says Frank. He doesn't want something like this to happen again.

Just then Ruth and Walter come into Frank's room. "We won't stay long," says Ruth.

"That's OK," says Marge. "We were just talking about money."

Would you talk about money problems with friends?

Frank won't give up everything

Walter, come here a minute. There's a $10 bill in the drawer. Don't let Marge see you.

Yes, it's here.

I want you to get me as many 60¢ cigars as that will buy. I can't give up everything. After all, I already gave up my gall bladder.

Ruth and Marge talk to each other. Frank calls Walter over to him. "There is a $10 bill over there," Frank says. "Will you get it, please? Don't let Marge see you."

Walter finds the money. "Take that $10 bill," says Frank, "and get me as many 60¢ cigars as possible. I can't give up everything! I already gave up my gall bladder!"

If you had to save money, how would you do it?